HERO JOURNALS

Hannibal of Carthage

Sean Stewart Price

Raintree is an imprint of Capstone Global Library Limited, a company incorporated in England and Wales having its registered office at 7 Pilgrim Street, London, EC4V 6LB – Registered company number: 6695582

www.raintreepublishers.co.uk
myorders@raintreepublishers.co.uk

Text © Capstone Global Library Limited 2014
First published in hardback in 2014
Paperback edition first published in 2015
The moral rights of the proprietor have been asserted.

Edited by Adam Miller, Charlotte Guillain, and Claire Throp
Designed by Richard Parker and Ken Vail Graphic Design
Original illustrations © Capstone Global Library Ltd 2014
Illustrated by [illustrator name]
Picture research Tracy Cummins
Production by Victoria Fitzgerald
Originated by Capstone Global Library Ltd
Printed and bound in China by CTPS

ISBN 978 1 406 26570 5 (hardback)
17 16 15 14 13
10 9 8 7 6 5 4 3 2 1

ISBN 978 1 406 26577 4 (paperback)
18 17 16 15 14
10 9 8 7 6 5 4 3 2 1

British Library Cataloguing in Publication Data
Price, Sean Stewart
Hannibal of Carthage. – (Hero journals)
937'.04'092-dc23
A full catalogue record for this book is available from the British Library.

Acknowledgements
We would like to thank the following for permission to reproduce photographs: Art Resource, NY pp. 10 (Alfredo Dagli Orti/The Art Archive), 18 (Gianni Dagli Orti/The Art Archive), 21 (Alfredo Dagli Orti), 23 (DeA Picture Library), 38 (Scala); Bridgemann pp. 13 (Giraudon), 14 (© Look and Learn), 16 (© Look and Learn), 27 (Universal History Archive/UIG), 28 (De Agostini Picture Library/G. Dagli Orti), 29 (Giovanni Battista Tiepolo), 33 (Giulio Romano), 39 (Alinari); Corbis pp. 7 (© Roger Wood), 37 (© Corbis); Getty Images pp. 4 (Hulton Archive), 9 (DEA/M. Carrieri/De Agostini), 22 (Time Life Pictures/Mansell/Time Life Pictures); Shutterstock pp. 30 (Pawel Kowalczyk), 35 (Nataliya Hora); Superstock pp. 5 (Universal Images Group), 6 (DeAgostini), 32 (Pantheon). Design features reproduced with permission of Shutterstock (R-studio, Pavel K, Picsfive, karawan).

Cover photograph of Hannibal reproduced with permission of Pantheon (SuperStock).

Contents

War and revenge

I, Hannibal Barca, have a story to tell you. A story of adventure and daring, loyalty, and betrayal. However, the ending has not turned out the way I'd planned. I had hoped to tell you about how I defeated and humiliated Rome. I wanted to tell you how I raised Carthage to be master of the Mediterranean Sea.

And I almost reached that dream. As a general, my crushing victories against Rome rewrote history. But my defeats off the battlefield cost me everything. I fled, but have now run out of places to hide. The Romans have tracked me down. They will kill me or lead me back in chains if they can.

But they'll never catch me alive. And first I will tell my story.

There are many paintings and drawings of me. But none was done during my lifetime.

Who were the Carthaginians?

Carthage was founded in the 800s BC by the Phoenicians from modern-day Lebanon. The Phoenicians are widely credited with inventing the alphabet. They were great sea traders, and this helped spread the use of alphabets. Phoenicians also set up colonies, like Carthage, around the Mediterranean Sea.

The Punic Wars

Rome and Carthage (which is now part of Tunisia) fought three wars over a period of about 118 years. They struggled for control of the Mediterranean Sea. These wars are remembered as the "Punic" wars. *Punic* is another word for "Phoenician".

First Punic War 264–241 BC
Hannibal's father, Hamilcar, led the Carthaginian forces during this war. Like Hannibal, he was a brilliant general.

Second Punic War 218–201 BC
Could Hannibal's clever leadership defeat Rome?

Third Punic War 149–146 BC
Hannibal's family was no longer around for this war.

My youth

I was born in Carthage in 247 BC. I am the son of a great general, Hamilcar Barca. My family is wealthy and powerful like Carthage itself. The city is built on a cliff in North Africa overlooking the Mediterranean Sea. It sits on a sloping hillside. At the top of the hill are all the city's most important buildings and temples.

About 700,000 people live here, many on the hillside. The roads leading up the hill are narrow. Many houses have shops facing the dirt streets. Bedrooms and other living rooms are behind the shops. Some buildings are six storeys high.

Carthage became a great city because it is a port. Its ships trade all over the Mediterranean Sea. This makes the city very rich.

6

Carthaginians are skilled farmers, producing all kinds of crops: barley, figs, and olives. They are also great traders and sailors. Our navy was the strongest around — until the Romans came along.

I had the very best of everything. But my father wanted more than wealth and power. He was still angry about losing the First Punic War and longed to destroy Rome. I spent much of my life preparing to carry out my father's revenge.

Human sacrifice

Hannibal was the oldest son in his family. In Carthage, that could be dangerous. In times of trouble, Carthaginians sacrificed their children to the chief gods, Baal Hammon and his wife, Tanit. First-born sons of wealthy and powerful people were considered the greatest sacrifice for a city. To lose them showed great love to the gods. The Romans also practised human sacrifice and sometimes buried people alive after a bad military defeat. Like the Carthaginians, they did it to soothe the anger of the gods.

Children are sometimes sacrificed to the gods of Carthage. Rome also uses human sacrifice sometimes.

Raising lion cubs

KEY

- Zone under Carthaginian domination 218 BC
- Zone under Roman domination 218 BC
- → Hannibal's route

Carthage and Rome are the two strongest powers in the western Mediterranean Sea.

When I was nine years old, Carthage was at peace with Rome after the First Punic War. But my father was angry about Carthage's defeats. He took me to a religious temple and made me swear by the gods to "never show goodwill to the Romans".

Shortly after this, we went to live in Spain. We Carthaginians had conquered much of this territory, which was rich in gold and silver. We sold these precious metals to raise money for my father to rebuild Carthage's armies.

My father taught me and my brothers, Hasdrubal and Mago, all about war. He showed us how to use a sword and how to move an army. He also taught us that a good general understands his men. He sleeps on the ground with them and eats their bad food. Most of all, he fights by their side and shares their dangers. This forms an unbreakable bond.

"These are the lion cubs I'm rearing for the destruction of Rome."

Hamilcar Barca talking about his three sons

The thunderbolt brothers

Hannibal was given the last name *Barca* from his father. It means "thunderbolt". The name came from his father's ability to win lightning-quick victories during battle. According to legend, *Barca* lives on in the name of Barcelona, one of Spain's largest cities.

Hannibal's hero

Like most soldiers of his time, Hannibal's hero was Alexander the Great (right). About 80 years before Hannibal's birth, Alexander led a small army to defeat the much larger Persian Empire. Alexander was from Macedonia, which is part of modern-day Greece. His conquests spread Greek ideas and learning.

Taking charge

Fighting has raged around me all my life. That was also true in Spain. Some Spanish tribes resisted Carthaginian rule and fought against us. In 229 BC, when I was just 19 years old, my father died fighting against the Spaniards.

Most of my foot soldiers fight in heavy armour like this.

My father's army now needed a leader. As his oldest son, I might have been chosen. But I was too young. Instead, my brother-in-law Hasdrubal the Handsome was chosen.

Hasdrubal the Handsome continued my father's work. He conquered more of Spain, and I served as one of his generals. He also founded the city of New Carthage (now Cartagena in Spain) in 227 BC. That seaport city became the base of operations for me and my brothers.

Hasdrubal the Handsome kept peace with Rome, but only long enough to get our armies ready for the war everyone knew was coming. In 221 BC, he was murdered by a slave who had a grudge against him. Now 26 years old, I was chosen to replace him. The war with Rome was closer than ever.

Some soldiers — cavalry — fight on horseback. But most of the fighting is done by foot soldiers. Groups from opposite sides smash into each other on the battlefield.

"No sooner had Hannibal landed in Spain than he became a favourite with the whole army. The veterans thought they saw Hamilcar restored to them as he was in his youth; they saw the same determined expression, the same piercing eyes, the same cast of features."

Roman historian, Livy (59 BC– AD 17)

Document it!

When keeping a journal, include details like full names and dates. Also include things like sights, sounds, and smells. These will help you remember events later.

"We take war!"

The anger between Carthage and Rome finally boiled over because of the city of Saguntum. That city was an ally of Rome. But it was deep in Carthaginian territory in Spain.

The Romans often let their allies stir up trouble before coming to "rescue" them. I had no intention of letting that happen with Saguntum. My army surrounded the city and attacked it. The siege took eight months. Saguntum kept asking Rome for help. But the Romans did not think my troops could win. It was the first of many times that the Romans underestimated me.

Who ruled Carthage?

Carthage's government was an oligarchy. That means a small group controlled it. The main ruling body was the Council of Elders, made up of a few hundred wealthy men. The city was actually run by two "suffetes" or judges, who were elected each year. If the suffetes and council agreed on something, it became law. If they didn't agree, then an assembly of the people decided it. Any ordinary person could speak or propose changes at this assembly. During most of the Second Punic War, Hannibal's family members seem to have controlled Carthage's government. But they had many opponents.

The Romans did not believe that I could take Saguntum, partly because it sits high on a hill.

Crossing the Alps

The Romans prepared to send their armies to Spain. But I had no intention of waiting for them. Instead, I led my army across the Alps. The Alps are mountains in northern Italy. The Romans were not expecting an attack — let alone one from the north.

But the Alps are treacherous. It's hard for even a small group of men to cross them safely, and I wanted to send an army of 100,000 men and thousands of animals.

My march across the Alps was daring and dangerous. The Romans were not expecting an attack from these high mountains.

My men were not used to the bitterly cold weather. And the thin mountain air made it hard to breathe. High mountain paths were narrow and would sometimes collapse, sending men plunging to their deaths. There was also little food. If my guides became lost, the entire army could starve.

I knew about these and other dangers. But I also knew that my army was up to it. And I knew that if this worked, I might catch the Romans unprepared. That would ensure my legacy as the greatest warrior in history — even greater than Alexander the Great.

An army of mercenaries

Carthage did not have a large population. To find enough soldiers for the army, generals like Hannibal hired mercenaries. These soldiers fight only for pay. Mercenaries were common in the ancient world. But they were not seen as good soldiers. Many showed no loyalty. In many cases, the other side paid them to avoid fighting. That was not the case with Hannibal's mercenaries. His soldiers remained extremely loyal. They never rebelled against him, despite years of toil and danger.

Death in the snow

Crossing the Alps was even worse than I thought it would be. Thousands of men could not face the horrors of that march and turned back to Spain. Others died along the way. But the army pushed on.

Cold temperatures and snowy ground made life miserable. Yet I was able to get tens of thousands of men across the Alps into Italy.

The Gauls were the biggest threat. They were people who lived throughout France and northern Italy, including the Alps. Some Gauls were friendly. In fact, many joined my army. Others could be bought off with gifts. But others saw my army as a tempting target.

One group of Gauls pretended friendship and offered us guides through the mountain passes. But the guides led us into a giant ambush. In one attack, our war elephants saved the army. The Gauls had never seen such large animals. They ran in terror when they saw the giant beasts coming at them. This allowed my men to escape.

Of the 100,000 men who started with me, about 26,000 made it to Italy five months later. The rest deserted or died. But my army was tested by hardship and ready to kill Romans.

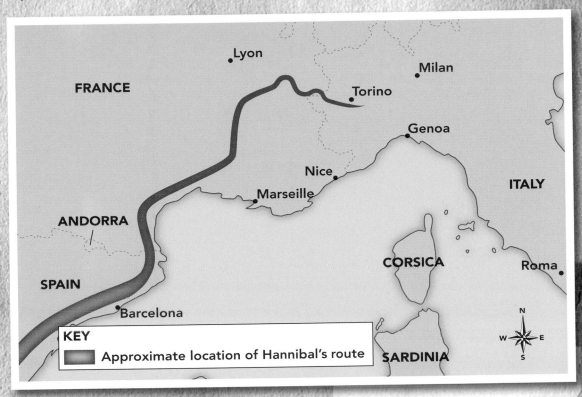

Map showing: FRANCE, Lyon, Milan, Torino, Genoa, Nice, Marseille, ITALY, ANDORRA, SPAIN, CORSICA, Roma, Barcelona, SARDINIA

KEY
Approximate location of Hannibal's route

Nobody is sure of my exact path through the Alps. This map shows one of the most likely routes.

War elephants

In the ancient world, many nations saw war elephants as the ultimate weapon. They could look terrifying to soldiers who had never seen them, like the Gauls. Also, horses did not like the smell of elephants and often panicked around them. But elephants really weren't that helpful on the battlefield. Romans learned to attack elephants from the sides with javelins and flaming objects, which caused the elephants to panic and stomp on friend and foe alike.

17

Rome learns to fear me

When the Romans learned of my march across the Alps, they were itching to fight. One Roman commander couldn't wait to do battle. But I forced him to march his men through the freezing Trebia River in December to get at me. Then I lured his troops to a spot where my cavalry, led by my brother Mago, lay in ambush. Any Romans not killed fled home.

I proudly shared the hard life of my soldiers. But when I was ill, I had to travel on an elephant in order to recover.

But the march south into Italy was difficult. At one point, we marched for three days and nights through a swamp. I became ill but there was nowhere to lie down so I travelled on an elephant — the only one to survive the long journey so far. The illness cost me my sight in one eye.

In June 217 BC, I lured another Roman commander to march his men near Lake Trasimene. The marching Romans had water on one side and hills on the other — the perfect place for an ambush!

The Romans had no idea my men were above them in the hills hidden by a heavy morning fog. I gave the order and my men came screaming down on the surprised Romans. Almost the entire Roman army — 15,000 men — were killed. Another 6,000 were captured.

The Romans were forced to flee and ended up in the lake!

"*Most of them were cut to pieces in marching order, as they were quite unable to protect themselves. … [Others] were forced into the lake in a mass, some of them quite lost their wits, and trying to swim in their armour, were drowned.*"

Roman historian, Polybius (200–118 BC)

The Delayer

After the Battle of Lake Trasimene, mothers and wives wailed in the streets of Rome for the husbands and sons who would never come home. No Romans were more shocked than the wealthy men who made up the Roman Senate. The Senate governed Rome. Senators held a drawn-out meeting to find a solution to my invasion.

Their solution? They elected a dictator. Under Roman law, he had absolute power to rule Rome for just one year. Then he had to give up power. The dictator they chose was Fabius Maximus. This was bad news. Unlike most Romans, Fabius Maximus understood me. He knew that my main problem was feeding my huge army.

Rome is ruled by a small group of wealthy men. The decisions they make in the Senate direct Rome's destiny.

So Fabius Maximus attacked my food supply. He destroyed all crops and livestock in the path of my army. He also attacked the small groups I sent out to look for food. But he refused to face me in open battle. He wanted to let hunger drive me from Italy.

This might have worked, too. But other Romans found this strategy humiliating. Rome's army was its pride and joy. Romans wanted to beat me in battle, not starve me out. My spies in Rome told me all about this. So I waited for Fabius Maximus' term as dictator to end. Once it did, I knew the Romans would come after me with their biggest army ever.

Quintus Fabius Maximus

Romans sneeringly called Fabius Maximus the *Cunctator*, which means "The Delayer". They scorned his way of dealing with Hannibal. This led directly to Rome's greatest military disaster – the Battle of Cannae.

Cannae

The Romans put together a force of 80,000 men. It was the largest Roman army ever assembled. On 2 August 216 BC, they caught up with me at the town of Cannae. My army had also grown, thanks to new recruits who had joined along the way. I now had about 35,000 men.

My spies were excellent. And I know how to think like my opponent. In this case, the Roman general against me was Varro. I knew that he would focus his troop at the centre of my line. He wanted to split my army in two. So I set up my line to give way in the middle — very slowly. Once the Romans pushed far enough, the two sides of my army would collapse on the middle around the Romans. Meanwhile, my horsemen would ride around the rear. The Romans would be completely surrounded.

At Cannae, tens of thousands of Romans were packed into a small area. My soldiers surrounded them and cut them down.

Cannae was a perfect place for a battle. Armies need flat ground so that soldiers can march side-by-side in giant formations.

That's what happened. Within minutes, more than 45,000 Romans were cut off. They were packed in an area of less than 2.5 square kilometres. The weather was brutally hot, especially in heavy armour. Most had no water. Some simply gave up or passed out from the heat. Others fought viciously to the end. A handful escaped.

Deadly day at Cannae

The Battle of Cannae remained the bloodiest day in European history until World War I, more than 2,000 years later. More than 48,000 Romans and about 8,000 Carthaginians died. After the battle, Hannibal's forces took about 10,000 Romans as prisoners. They were sold off as slaves in Greece. This was common for prisoners of war at that time.

How to use a victory

After Cannae, Rome was within my grasp. Some of my generals urged me to march on Rome. One of my cavalry commanders, Maharbal, said, "Follow me. I will go first with the cavalry, that the Romans may know that you are there before they even know you are coming."

He had a point. My spies in Rome said that the city was in panic. Everyone was afraid that Hannibal was at the gates. The Romans even sacrificed young people to ease the anger of the gods. The Senate frantically built a new army from jailed criminals and freed slaves.

Even so, I hesitated. Rome was still heavily defended. And the Romans remained determined to fight. I might destroy my army taking the city. Also, Rome had other armies abroad. If one of them appeared, I could be in trouble.

That's why other generals argued for an indirect approach. After the victory at Cannae, other major Italian cities, like Capua, were joining our cause. Without friends, Rome would have to give up.

I chose the indirect approach. Those who wanted to march on Rome never forgave me. "So the gods have not given everything to one man," Maharbal said. "You know how to win a victory, Hannibal, but you don't know how to use one."

Later I realized how right he was.

Document it!

When writing a journal, try to include dialogue from conversations you have heard or participated in.

The spoils of victory

After Cannae, Carthaginians prised gold rings off the bodies of Roman senators and noblemen who died. Hannibal had hundreds of these rings after the battle.

The gold rings that my men took off the Romans at Cannae helped me win over allies. They showed just how many Romans I had defeated.

Stalemate and decline

After the losses at Cannae, the Romans returned to Fabius' strategy of delay and harassment. I still won battles and destroyed their armies. But the Romans just replaced them with more.

Fighting continued for more than five years.

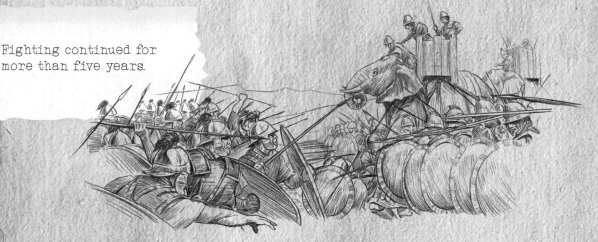

The Romans also attacked anyone in Italy who sided with me. Five years after Cannae, in 211 BC, the Romans threatened to take back Capua. I marched on Rome to try to distract them but they had learned to ignore my tricks. Capua fell and everyone there was killed or sold into slavery.

Meanwhile, I realized that I had no chance of actually taking Rome. The Romans were too strong, and Carthage had done little to reinforce my army. My political enemies now controlled the Council of Elders there. They opposed the war and left me to fight on my own.

So I retreated to southern Italy. From now on, the war would only get worse for me and Carthage.

Fighting elsewhere

The Second Punic War was not just fought on the Italian peninsula. Carthaginian armies also fought in Sicily and Spain. In Sicily, the major target for Rome was the pro-Carthaginian city of Syracuse. The city's defence was led by Archimedes, a Greek scientist. He invented clever machines that destroyed Roman ships. One of them was a crane that picked up ships and then dropped them, causing them to sink. These devices helped Syracuse hold out for months. But a Roman soldier killed Archimedes when Syracuse finally fell in 212 BC.

Document it!

Be consistent with your journal. Write every day and soon you'll have a lot of entries.

Archimedes' "claw" helped defend Syracuse against the Romans. These machines — and others — struck terror into the Romans.

Rome finds my equal

While I fought in Italy, my brothers Hasdrubal and Mago held the fort in Spain. Spain was very important to me. The silver and gold there paid for my soldiers. The Romans had sent armies to seize control of Spain. But my brothers had defeated each one.

Then in 209 BC, the Romans sent Scipio. He was young and untested. The only reason he got the job was because no other Roman general wanted it. But Scipio had learned from me to do the unexpected. He launched an attack on my Spanish operation at the city of New Carthage. This caught everyone by surprise. The city fell with barely a fight.

Publius Cornelius Scipio Africanus

As a teenager, Scipio rescued his father from certain death in a battle against Hannibal. Scipio was also one of the few Roman soldiers to escape from Cannae. He lost relatives, including his father, in fighting against Hannibal. All this taught Scipio to fight like Hannibal, with trickery. He used that knowledge to conquer Spain from the Carthaginians and then to threaten their homeland.

Scipio was one of the few Romans who understood how to beat me.

Next, he beat my brothers in battle, driving them out of Spain. Hasdrubal tried to come to Italy to help me. But he was caught and killed. I didn't know he was dead until the Romans catapulted his head into my camp. As I stood there looking at it, I realized that we had lost. I had won victory after victory and it hadn't mattered. My time in Italy was almost done.

The Romans were cruel and catapulted my brother's head towards me to let me know they had won.

Defending Carthage

By 204 BC, the Romans were winning on all fronts. My armies in Italy were surrounded and couldn't move. Meanwhile, Scipio took the war directly to Carthage by invading North Africa.

Scipio's army quickly smashed the Carthaginian forces. Carthage's Council of Elders begged Scipio for peace. Scipio knew that Carthage was still well defended. Attacking it successfully could take years. He wanted credit for ending the war, and he needed to do it quickly. So he agreed to give Carthage generous terms.

I left the metal tablet describing my victories in a temple like this one.

At this point, I found out that my brother Mago had died of wounds he had suffered in battle. Of the three "lions" that my father had raised to fight Rome, only I remained. Meanwhile, Carthage's Council of Elders ordered me to return home immediately.

I had been in Italy for 15 years. The Romans had never defeated me. But they had learned to ignore my victories and keep attacking. Before I left, I ordered a metal tablet to be created that described my victories. The tablet was placed in the temple of the goddess Hera. The Romans dared not touch it without angering the goddess. Then I packed up my army and we sailed home.

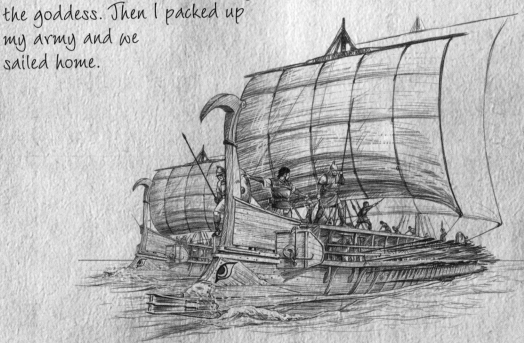

"Gnashing his teeth and groaning, and scarcely keeping back the tears, [Hannibal] listened to the words of the emissaries [from the Council of Elders]. After they had delivered their instructions, he exclaimed, 'I am being recalled by men who, in forbidding the sending of reinforcements and money, were long ago trying to drag me back.'"

Roman historian, Livy (59 BC– AD 17)

The Battle of Zama

The truce between Carthage and Rome didn't last long. Some hungry Carthaginians raided Roman ships loaded with grain. The Romans demanded punishment. The Carthaginians refused. The war was back on.

I asked to meet Scipio before the Battle of Zama. More than any other Roman, he had ruined my plans. He was young, just 34 years to my 46. I reminded him that fortune was fickle. That he could lose everything with a defeat. All he had to do was renew the peace treaty. But Scipio refused, saying his cause was right.

I tried to talk Scipio (on the right) out of fighting at Zama. But our meeting could not stop this final battle.

By the time of Zama, the Romans had learned how to fight against my elephants. These animals did me little good.

Scipio's army was smaller than mine. He had only 29,000 men to my 50,000. But they were well trained and battle-tested. I still had my old veterans. But they made up only about one-third of the army. The rest were a mish-mash of new recruits and mercenaries.

The Battle of Zama was a slugging match. My veterans clashed for hours with Scipio's army. Nobody could tell how it would end. But then the Roman cavalry arrived. They crashed into my force from the rear — just as my horsemen had done to the Romans at Cannae. My old soldiers had never tasted defeat; they broke rank and ran.

"Upon [the Roman cavalry's] charging Hannibal's rear, the greater part of his men were cut down in their ranks. Of those who attempted to fly, very few escaped with their lives... On the Roman side there fell over 1,500; on the Carthaginian, over 20,000. The prisoners taken were almost as numerous."

Roman historian, Polybius (200–118 BC)

After the war

There was nothing left to do. I had to go to the Council of Elders and tell them to accept Scipio's peace terms. Some fools still wanted to carry on the fight. One elder stood up to argue for better terms. I knocked him down and silenced the rest. I told them it was unthinkable that anyone in Carthage did "not bless his stars that, now that he was at the mercy of the Romans, he has obtained such lenient terms."

Knocking down the elder made everyone else keep quiet.

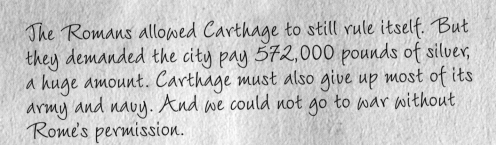

The Romans allowed Carthage to still rule itself. But they demanded the city pay 572,000 pounds of silver, a huge amount. Carthage must also give up most of its army and navy. And we could not go to war without Rome's permission.

Scipio was merciful to me. He could have dragged me back to Rome in chains. Why didn't he? I think he saw there was no need. Harsher terms would mean more fighting. And why fight when he had already won? His treaty stripped me of my ability to make war. Carthage was now a servant to Rome. And so was I.

But I was still popular with the people in Carthage, so I entered politics. I was named as a suffete, one of the men who ran the city. I kept taxes low and became a champion of the common people. I also stopped the bribery of officials that had been common for so long and gave people more power over the Council of Elders. All of these moves were very popular with ordinary people. But they made my enemies on the council angry.

Rome's revenge

Those enemies on the council wanted me out of Carthage.
So they told the Romans that I had plotted secretly with
Antiochus, a king in the Middle East and one of Rome's
enemies. It wasn't true. But Rome believed the rumour.
I knew that the Council of Elders was ready to hand me
over to the Romans. So in 195 BC, I crept away in the
dead of night.

By falsely accusing me of plotting with Antiochus, my
enemies had forced me to join him. I had nowhere else
to run. I did try to help Antiochus. But the Romans
defeated his armies in 191 BC. They promptly demanded
my surrender. I fled again.

I had to run like that several times over the next nine
years. Finally, I ended up under the protection of a minor
king in Turkey. My last military victory was helping him.
I told his soldiers to catapult clay pots of poisonous snakes
onto the enemy's ships. At first, they laughed at the idea.
But the snakes caused the enemy soldiers to panic, making
them easy to beat.

But the Romans are relentless. Again, they have
demanded my surrender. The king is about to give in but I
have decided to stop running. I am 64 years old and tired.
But I won't let the Romans get me. Instead, I will take
poison. Soon the Romans will be able to rest, for their
greatest enemy will be dead.

The Romans would not rest until I was dead. My victories over them were never forgotten — or forgiven.

"Let us free the Roman people from their long-standing anxiety, seeing that they find it tedious to wait for an old man's death."

Hannibal, 183 BC

Hannibal's legacy

Hannibal was one of the best military leaders in history. During his 16 fighting years in Italy and Spain, he never once lost a major battle. And he destroyed Roman armies five times. Today, soldiers still study his battles, especially his amazing victory at Cannae.

Carthage gained nothing by betraying Hannibal. The city had prospered, thanks in part to Hannibal's reforms. But Carthage's obedience and prosperity only angered Rome's most powerful senators. They were convinced that Carthage would attack Rome again. In 150 BC, the Romans started the Third Punic War. Four years later, Roman armies captured Carthage and destroyed it. Hundreds of thousands of people were killed. Another 50,000 were sold into slavery.

Many soldiers preferred to die in battle rather than be captured. Captivity meant slavery.

The end of Carthage marked the true beginning of the Roman Empire. With Carthage out of the way, Rome controlled the western Mediterranean Sea. Over the next 150 years, it would take control of the eastern Mediterranean, too. Rome's influence would shape law and culture all over the world for centuries to come.

But fear of Hannibal remained. Mothers frightened their children by saying "Hannibal's at the gates!" They meant that a blood-thirsty monster was about to get them. The legend of Hannibal would be burned in Roman memories forever.

Cato the Elder

Cato was a Roman senator. He accused Scipio Africanus of taking bribes. This probably wasn't true but it helped to force Scipio from Roman politics. Cato's deepest fear was that Carthage would become powerful again and threaten Rome. For years, every speech he made ended with the phrase, "Carthage must be destroyed!" Cato's hostility to Carthage helped lead to the Third Punic War.

Cato was also a political enemy of Scipio. In time, he drove Scipio from Rome because Scipio argued for treating Carthage — and Hannibal — with mercy.

Timeline

264 BC Outbreak of the First Punic War between Carthage and Rome

247 Hannibal is born

241 First Punic War ends with a Roman victory. Carthage loses territory in Sicily to the Romans.

241–238 Carthage's mercenaries revolt because they have not been paid. Hamilcar Barca, Hannibal's father, finally puts down the revolt.

237 While Carthage is weakened by the revolt, Rome takes more territory in Sardinia and Corsica

236–229 Hamilcar goes to Spain. He conquers territory and rebuilds his army. His family rules Spain in Carthage's name.

229 Hamilcar dies. His son-in-law, Hasdrubal the Handsome, takes power in Spain.

227 Hasdrubal founds New Carthage in Spain

226 Hasdrubal reaches treaty with Rome

221 Hasdrubal is murdered. Hannibal's army names him leader of the armies in Spain.

219 Hannibal begins the siege of Saguntum

218 Rome and Carthage begin the Second Punic War. Hannibal sets out to cross the Alps. Late in the year, he wins the battles, including one at the Trebia River.

217 Hannibal wins the Battle of Lake Trasimene. Fabius Maximus is named dictator of Rome for one year.

216	Hannibal wins the Battle of Cannae, his biggest victory. The Roman city of Capua takes sides with Hannibal. So do other cities.
212	Other major cities begin to side with Hannibal. Rome begins the effort to retake Capua. The Sicilian city of Syracuse falls to the Romans.
211	Hannibal marches on Rome but cannot take the city. Capua falls to the Romans.
209	Scipio captures New Carthage in Spain
208	Scipio drives out the last of Carthage's armies from Spain
207	Hannibal's brother Hasdrubal is killed in battle
206	Hannibal is bottled up in southern Italy. Scipio continues to defeat other Carthaginian armies.
204	Scipio invades North Africa. He wins victories against Carthage and its allies.
203	Hannibal is recalled from Italy
202	Hannibal faces his first major defeat at the Battle of Zama
201	The Second Punic War ends
196	Hannibal elected as suffete of Carthage
195	Hannibal forced to flee Carthage
183	Hannibal kills himself to avoid being captured by the Romans. Scipio also dies.
150	Rome decides to go to war against Carthage. Third Punic War begins.
146	The Romans capture and destroy Carthage

Write your own journal

Creating a journal is very personal. The words you put down in it reflect what you think and do. But the way you put it together also says something about you. It can be as simple as putting words on paper. Or those words can be illustrated with art and photographs. These can make it more interesting, and can help you tell a better story. Here are some steps to help you create the best possible scrapbook or journal.

1. **Gather supplies.** Think about what you'd like your journal to look like. You can do it in the form of a scrapbook. If you are struggling to come up with ideas, ask a friend or relative. You can also look online with your teacher's help. Then come up with the supplies you'll need to make your scrapbook. They might include things like glue, scissors, a ruler, drawing pencils, and so on.

2. **Think of three topics to write about.** They can be anything: perhaps a funny story about your pet, or describing how you got in and out of trouble. Write down your ideas on a separate sheet of paper. Then start to write your stories in your journal.

3. **Do one entry a day.** It's important to keep writing in your journal. But you only have so much time each day, so don't try to write down everything that comes to you. Pick the most important event or thought and write about it. If you have time to write more, that's great. If not, at least you've written something – even if it's just one sentence.

4. Look for ways to illustrate. If you're good at drawing, you could make sketches, like the one below and the others found in this book. If not, maybe print out art or photos you see on the internet that illustrate what you're saying.

5. Remember that there are no rules. This is your journal! Make what you want out of it.

Glossary

Alps mountain range in Europe, crossed by Hannibal to invade Italy. The mountains stretch for about 1,200 kilometres (745 miles).

ambush sudden, unexpected attack

anxiety great concern

base of operations place for an army to rest and gather supplies

catapult ancient weapon that hurls stones and heavy objects long distances

cavalry soldiers who fight on horseback

Council of Elders key part of Carthage's government

determined unwilling to give up

emissary representative

fickle when a person or organization changes their mind a lot

found start or begin something, such as a city or organization

gnash grind together or bite

god object of worship

goddess female god

humiliate greatly embarrass

lenient merciful or tolerant

mercenary soldier who fights for money rather than something he or she believes in

panic sudden, overwhelming fear

Phoenician ancient people from modern-day Lebanon who founded Carthage

precious metal extremely valuable metal, such as gold or silver

Punic another word for "Phoenician"

recall ask or demand to return

reinforce strengthen or support

sacrifice something of great value given to a god or goddess

Senate ruling body of ancient Rome

slave person owned by someone else. A slave has to work for no money or other reward.

spoils goods or property seized after a victory

suffete two suffetes, or judges, ruled over Carthage for one-year terms

treacherous difficult and dangerous

veteran experienced soldier

Find out more

Books

Hannibal: Great General of the Ancient World (Rulers of the Ancient World), Karen Clemens Warrick (Enslow, 2006)

Hannibal: Rome's Worst Nightmare (Wicked History), Philip Brooks (Franklin Watts, 2009)

Romans (Tony Robinson's Weird World of Wonders), Tony Robinson (Macmillan, 2012)

Websites

www.history.com/topics/hannibal
This website has lots of videos, audio, and photos about Hannibal.

www.phoenicia.org
This website has lots of information on Canaan/Phoenicia and its people.

Place to visit

British Museum
Great Russell Street
London
WC1B 3DG

www.britishmuseum.org
The British Museum contains some interesting objects from Carthage, including some coins from Hannibal's time.

Topics for further research

- Rome and Carthage controlled the western Mediterranean Sea. But other civilizations shared the Mediterranean. What were they? Pick one and find out what life was like there during the time of the Punic Wars.

- Warfare in ancient times was very different from how it is today. Leaders often refused to let their army fight if they thought the gods were against them. Many battles began with religious ceremonies. Find out how religious beliefs influenced ancient attitudes towards fighting.

- The Romans eventually defeated Carthage and destroyed it. But Carthage was later rebuilt. What was the "second" Carthage like, who ruled it, and how long did it last?

Index